To Joann,-

May your heart be filled
with joy, always.

Apex, NC June 1ST 2005

Grains of Sand and Murmurs of the Sea

A Collection of Poems and Selected Essays

By

Joseph Cione

authorHOUSE™

1663 LIBERTY DRIVE, SUITE 200
BLOOMINGTON, INDIANA 47403
(800) 839-8640
WWW.AUTHORHOUSE.COM

First published by AuthorHouse 08/26/04

ISBN: 1-4184-9657-X (sc)

Printed in the United States of America
Bloomington, Indiana

This book is printed on acid-free paper.

To Sara,
devoted wife,
faithful friend,
and loving mother
of a lifetime.

TABLE OF CONTENTS

A grain of sand
is a tiny, gritty particle
of silica.
It has no pretense.
It feeds on sunshine
and murmurs of the sea.
Children build
their castles with it.
My verses
are tiny, living fibers
of my heart,
beckoning a world
I once knew,
as they echo
the eager yearnings
of my soul.

~ POEMS ~

SEASONAL MUSINGS

Memories
of lost fragrances,
promises of new ones,
and whispers
of eternity.

Luscious gowns parading
upon nature's stage,
bearing fruit
and tastes of honey.

A listless moon,
like a bored puppy,
staring
into the tedium
of a frozen tundra.

Spent leaves
nudged by the breeze
dancing
in the cool air,
flaunting its magic
of color and beauty.

REFLECTIONS

When the willingness to pursue
the "ought" is replaced by the
insolence to secure the "want,"
freedom becomes an empty word,
and nothing more.

Clamoring for "rights" while
ignoring "responsibilities,"
flies in the face of reason.
Responsibility is the only thread
with which all the "rights" are
woven into the fabric of the

When I see a weed
push through a crack
in a walkway,
I stop and gaze at it
n wonder.
What perseverance!
human heart.

When I watch a butterfly
flutter its wings
over a field of blooming flowers,
I can't help thinking
if all the atheists are blind.

Within the concept of eternity,
our life span is shorter than
the wink of an eye.
Yet, we go out of our way
to waste it in the senseless
pursuit of self-gratification
and greed

In all the high schools
of America, any student
has the right to request
and receive a free condom.
The same student does
not have the right
to recite aloud a prayer
within the school building.

WHEN ROSES BLOOM

Rose was her name.
She bloomed in the shade,
alone,
among thorns.
Soft were her petals
and her fragrance sweet.
She bloomed for many a spring,
yearning to see but only a gleam
and feel the warmth
of the noonday sun.
One cold, wintry day
her petals withered
and her fragrance left with the wind.
At every spring,
when roses bloom,
I see Mother in every rose
that blooms free,
kissed by the sun.
And I rejoice
as I breathe once again
the sweetness of her fragrance.

SARA'S HANDS

Small,
nimble,
loving hands,
they're Sara's hands.
As I hold them within my own,
I delight
in the glow of countless memories:
Bursts of sunshine,
passing clouds,
sighs,
tears
and peals of laughter.
As I gaze at them,
I see endless chores,
in every line,
in every crease,
and tender touches
that brushed many a tear away.
I see a loving care
that never ceased
for anyone, anytime, anywhere.
Now, in their golden years,
Sara's hands never stopped
loving,
caring,
praying,
for anyone,
anytime,
anywhere.

MEMORIES

Like a roving bird
fleeing the cold,
longing for warmer shores,
I too, at times,
weary of the frigid moods of winter,
set my mind on nimble wings
and let it wander
across my world of fading memories,
fragments of time
teeming with faces and sounds
I once knew,
tasty bites of familiar fares,
dazzling gleams of the scorching sun,
cooling offerings from the restless sea,
familiar fragrances of spring
riding the morning breeze.
And I live,
as my heart rests,
cuddled,
within the warm embrace
of time.

THE INTRUDERS

They stand barefooted on the side of a dusty road,

holding an empty bowl.

And they stare into our home

with eyes that lay bare the hunger that gnaws within.

They are Africa's children.

We look at them, as they intrude upon our daily comfort.

And we send them away,

instantly,

with a flick of a finger,

from the cozy world we call our own.

But the empty bowls

and the painful stares

have a way of lingering,

amidst our abundance and our frivolous wants.

It is good that they do, as they ought,

to awake in us the will to find an answer to the questions:

Who are our brothers and our sisters?

How can we help them?

THE CEREMONY

A woman dressed in black
stands at attention,
a hand pressed against her heart.
Men in uniform stand with her,
saluting a memory.
The woman's eyes stare
into the distance,
perhaps to a hallowed ground
moist with the blood
of her son.
A coffin rests on a stand.
A burst of gunfire echoes through the air
to honor the dead.
A flag is carefully folded
to comfort the living.
Drums start their cadence
as the coffin slowly sinks
into an open grave.
And the ceremony ends.

WHERE IS GOD?

Where is your God?
-was the angry question.-
Pain and strife I only see
and malice too cruel to mention!
Try to seek Him, came the reply,
with a pure heart and faith unbound
and you will surely find Him
and recognize Him all around.
You'll see God every morning
in the splendor of the rising sun,
you'll see Him again
when the day is done.
And if you gaze upon the sky
deep and very far
You'll see God again
in the twinkling of a star.
You'll see Him
in the fields filled with grain
and in the refreshing coolness
of a summer rain.
You'll see God even more
in the beauty of every flower,
and when the winter comes,
you'll see him in nature's awesome power.
And if you are grieving
for an illness or a sudden loss
you will surely find Him
hanging from the Cross.

PILGRIMS WE ALL ARE

No, it's not true,

we are not masters of our own destiny.

Nor are we conquerors,

haughty

and free

to plunder justice and truth.

Pilgrims we all are,

called upon to wander

briefly,

upon the testing grounds of righteousness,

toiling

side by side

on a tiny speck of the universe

called Earth.

Brothers we all are,

diverse, to be sure,

like flowers of the fields,

yes, diverse,

yet the same,

living,

hoping,

striving to bear our burdens,

and stumbling,

as we keep climbing

our mountains,

all the way to the top,

and beyond.

THE SAND CASTLE

A child,
kneeling on the wet sand,
is building his castle.
His nimble hands move quickly,
digging,
shaping,
pouring out of a pail,
and out of his heart,
the makings of a dream.
Walls, moats, towers
emerge from the sand.
His eyes sparkle
as he steps back
and stands motionless,
smiling
at the work of his hands.
Suddenly,
a wave surges from the sea,
rushes through with a gurgling sound
and crashes into the castle.
The child reels back
as he watches the receding wave
taking back to the sea
the formless remnants of his dream.
The child glares at the sea
as he cries out:
Why?... why?...why?

THE RIGHT TO BE

A seed sprouts,
beneath a broken slab.
A tender stem climbs,
unafraid,
through the jagged edges,
bent by the valiant effort,
yearning
to see the light of the sun.
It's a weed,
straightening its stem
proudly,
and shouting to all creation:
Here I am!
Here I am!

MEETING BERNIE

We sat quietly,
in the familiar place,
waiting to hear
words of wisdom and truth.
A man called Bernie,
a Cistercian monk,
burst through the screen
like a hot sun in the height of winter,
walked into our hearts
and managed to stay there
for the evening and beyond.
Joy lived in Bernie's heart,
and humility was his companion.
His words were a healing balm
and his laughter a refreshing breeze,
bringing light into musty corners
and life into stale attitudes.
He found God everywhere.
He found Him in the loftiness
of a mountain range
and in the simple quaintness of a daisy,
in the colorful spectacle
of a sunrise
and in the soothing sound
of a rushing brook.
He lived each day of his life
sharing the love song
he bore within his soul.
Suddenly,

his love song was heard no more
and his heart withered,
like a blooming flower
torn from its stem.
We sat quietly
in the familiar place.
There was nothing else for us
to see or hear.
We had already seen the face of TRUTH
and heard the voice of WISDOM.

THE UMPIRE

He travels across the land,

often trudging through lonely places,

yearning for home.

He always works

under the scrutiny

of an unfriendly crowd,

around a place called "diamond."

There, he rules over three "bases"

and a plate called "home"

where he is expected to judge

fairly,

and within a blink

all that opened-eyes can't see.

With boldness

and a dash of flair, he roars:

STRIKE! BALL! FOUL!

according to his view.

Besides, he can call a runner OUT!

while another may slide in SAFE!

Regardless.

Upon his head

is bound to fall the ire of many.

No matter.

Amid the whining and the cursing,

the spitting and the griping

he usually endures.

In the end,

he is able to walk away from it all,

tired and lonely,

to seek comfort

in the cuddly embrace

of a warm shower.

LIFE SENTENCE

I saw Jim

through a web of steel bars,

handcuffed

and with shackles on his feet.

A steel door opened and closed

with a thump.

I watched him shuffle in

and slump onto a stool.

Our eyes met, without a word.

He probed mine with a stare.

"Hi! I am Jim-he said-

Thanks for the visit.

I am innocent,

I raped no one!"

His voice rose with every word,

and his eyes poured into mine

a measure of his pain.

I saw tears in them

as he spoke of bitterness and pain.

In the end,

I could only offer Him

the hollow sound of words.

The steel door opened again,

a guard called his name

and Jim resumed his shuffle,

back to his cell

and to the lonely sound of silence.

Outside, the air felt heavy,

and the sun shone cold,

amid a murky sky.

A FLEETING MOMENT

I stand at the edge of a pond,
intruding
upon nature's splendor.
I watch naked branches
reaching for the sky
like eager arms
wanting to embrace the sun,
spent leaves,
faded remnants of autumn's glory,
gathering meekly
into a restless heap
shaped by the breeze,
and the morning sun,
filtering through the quivering branches
as it paints a web
on the liquid canvas of the pond.
I hear a croaking cadence
from the rocks,
followed by a moaning screech
from the crow's perch.
Nature breathes,
as I do,
and her heart throbs with mine
as I share but a fleeting moment
in the eternal pulse
of time.

FLUTTERING ARROGANCE

It appeared suddenly,

flaunting its hues,

fluttering

over a field of blooming possibilities.

It chose an unsuspecting pansy,

and it began to glut

over the luscious fare.

Then, flapping its wings,

it swayed over a daisy

and onto a petunia,

and, finally, onto a buttercup.

When it had its fill,

it floated away,

to disappear behind a bush,

to rest and dream

of soft petals and sweet honey drops

plundered

in the heat of a summer day.

Joseph Cione

THE CHAMPIONS

They came,

from the streets of Maracaibo

to the lush fields of Pennsylvania,

the Boys of Venezuela,

with hope in their heart

and smiles on their faces.

They came to play

the American Game

sharing but one bat among all.

No matter.

They hit, they ran, they scored,

flaunting their skills with exuberant flair.

In the end,

they triumphed

over the American boys from Texas,

and they rejoiced

with the kind of zest

that only the young can know.

Beyond the mountains of Pennsylvania

and across the sea,

a whole nation celebrated

and hailed

their heroes,

the Boys of Maracaibo,

who came to share one bat

and returned home

sharing in the reality

of one dream.

SUNSHINE

Floating
like a dazzling balloon on a string,
a new sun rises
painting the sky
with hues of pink and gold
and shades of fire.
As I watch nature's splendor,
deep from within it,
I seem to hear
God's voice,
for all to hear:
"Let there be light
and warmth
and life to the fullest
to all who hope and dream.
I make the sun shine
on the tallest tree
and on the smallest weed."

THE CHILDREN OF BAGHDAD

On a street of Baghdad,

children's voices tinkle

as silver bells,

as they giggle and play

on the cobblestones.

Anxious eyes watch them

behind window shades.

Suddenly,

the weapons roar

and innocent blood

splatters

on the cobblestones.

The giggles stop,

and the wails begin to rise

beyond the shattered street,

over the mountains

and across the oceans of the world.

No one hears them.

No one wants to hear them.

And the children's blood

continues to splatter

on the cobblestones.

THE MERCY PLACE

They come
everyday,
the needy,
with empty
hands,
bearing within
their hearts
the anguish
of hidden sorrows.
They knock, and the door swings open at the place where
Mercy lives,
amid a throng
of smiling Angels
of many names,
faces,
and assorted
wing spans,
ready and willing,
always,
to satisfy the hunger
and ease the pain,
today and always,
eager to share
the unquenchable
flame
of God's Love

23

CHILDREN

Children,

they bloom everywhere,

anytime,

in palaces and in slums,

bearing the same gifts of innocence and grace.

Their laughter rings clear,

like the rushing water

of a mountain stream.

They trust,

and they feel free to gaze into the face of truth

and smile.

They are God's

most generous gift

to humanity,

and the most precious.

....

And we kill them

in their mothers' womb,

everyday, everywhere

legally,

for a fee,

in the name of freedom,

convenience

and greed.

IT'S A DUCKS' WORLD

They hold their heads high
as they wander
across the icy waters of the pond,
the ducks.
Some are white, others black,
and some others flaunt
a fancy hue
of green and gold.
Long-necked,
short-necked,
big sized or small,
they keep wandering together
in the dead of winter,
across the length and width
of their domain,
searching together,
finding together,
surviving together,
through the ice and the cold,
the whites, the blacks,
and those in between,
sharing,
in peace,
the miracle of nature's bounty.

GOLD FROM WITHIN

He had already crossed the finish line,

striking gold,

in the Nagano's snow,

Bjorn Daehlle,

a man of legend,

accustomed to feats of glory.

Tired and out of breath,

he did not wish to rest,

nor did he choose to bask in the glitter of his fame.

He chose to wait,

to honor

another man's courage

and praise

the boldness of his dream.

He stood still,

waiting,

until Philip Boit, Kenia's son,

staggered past the finish line,

flashing a smile, warm and wide,

for all to see and understand.

Bjorn Daehlle saw it

and understood,

and rushed to shake the hand that never quit,

to pat the back that never bent.

Two men in the snow,

dissimilar,

yet the same

in the lofty realm

of honor and grace.

RAINSTORM

Lightning flash
and thunders burst
amid a murky sky.
Then comes the rain,
a teeming mass, pounding
on the rooftops,
gurgling
through the gutters,
rushing
to flood the streets,
while a brisk wind chatters
through the treetops.
A lonely sparrow,
shivering in his hiding place,
hardly shows his beak.
He waits.
A child,
his nose against a window pane,
looks up and sighs.
He waits.
He knows that the sun will shine again,
tomorrow.

AN EYE FOR AN EYE

She never heard her mother sing her a lullaby,

nor did ever feel her father's hand

lay softly upon her head.

Karla Faye Tucker

was only a child

when drugs sparked fire into her brain.

She was only a child

when evil men eased their lust upon her tender body.

And she drifted

into the evil paths of sorrow,

like a leaf blown by the wind.

Until one day,

shameless and bold, she used an iron pick

to still two peoples' hearts.

Karla Faye Tucker

died for her crime,

killed by the Men of Law,

who finally collected

their pound of flesh,

from a child,

who never heard her mother sing her a lullaby,

nor did ever feel her father's hand

lay softly upon her head.

THE PROPHECY

The crowd

has long gone.

The place

of the

Skull

looks

desolate

with empty crosses.

No more taunts, no more jeers, no more blasphemies,

only the howling of the wind echoes across the valley.

Mary weeps.

Within her arms,

a lifeless Jesus

bleeds

from many wounds;

and in the midst

of her anguish,

Mary hears again,

within her heart,

Simeon's words

of long ago:

"and your heart

shall be pierced

by a sword..

pierced

by a sword..

by a

sword..

29

THE PILGRIM POPE

They came from everywhere
in joyful throngs,
filled with the exuberance
only the young can know;
they sang,
they cheered,
they chanted words of love.
No, they did not come to see "rock stars"
strutting upon a stage,
nor did they want to hear
instruments blaring the latest tunes.
They came to see a man,
old and ailing,
walking slowly,
leaning on a cane,
whose hands trembled
as he spoke in halting whispers
words of love.
In the end,
the young rose,
chanting the man's name,
whose courage
they came to honor,
whose faith
they came to share,
the man,
burdened with pain,
whose healing words stirred
the conscience of the world.

ASHES

A log from an oak tree
is burning
as it lays upon a grate.
Sparks burst
as flames keep gnawing
steadily
at every fiber,
and the warmth they bear
takes the sting out of
the wintry air.
Soon, the log is no more
and the flames turn
into waning embers,
without warmth
or glow.
What remains are cold ashes,
destined to bear
the ultimate affront:
a whiskbroom
and a dustpan.

FALLING LEAVES

Like winter leaves,
pitted,
discolored,
decaying remnants
of our lost springs,
we keep falling
from the height of our conceit,
scattered
by the fickle wind
of our desires,
drawn downward
into the churning cauldron
of all our selfishness and greed,
sharing a common destiny:
The ultimate sound of silence.
And when the moment comes
to still our whispers,
only our deeds will remain,
as a legacy
of our existence
in this speck of cosmicdust
we call Earth.

THEY CALL IT ENTERTAINMENT

There is a road,

well-traveled and wide

that crosses the heart of America.

It's a freeway,

called ENTERTAINMENT.

It has no speed limits

nor does it post any signs of danger.

It has bumper guards

at every turn,

and they named them

CONSTITUTIONAL RIGHTS.

Like bees to a honeycomb,

the young swarm to that road,

only to breathe polluted air

that taints the mind

and soils the heart.

And when the Columbine anger bursts,

violence is what we reap,

and sorrow,

and pain..

There is a better road

to lead the children through;

it's narrow and steep,

where the walk is safe

and anger has no place to brood.

It's called DIVINE GUIDANCE.

Only there,

LOVE rears the heart

and FAITH guides it

all the way

to the end,

and beyond.

SONG OF SPRING

A robin came to rest
on a twig of holly,
outside my windowpane.
He aimed his beak at me
and stared,
as if to say:
Come fly with me!
I closed my eyes,
and I did begin to rise,
floating
upon a ray of sun.
I roamed through many valleys
bursting with life anew,
I soared over many mountains
dressed in hues of spring.
Nature reveled,
cuddled
within the warm embrace
of the morning sun.
Amid that stillness,
I could feel her heart throbbing
in unison with mine.
My friend had flown away.
He wanted me to hear alone
the Song of Spring.

THE KILLING FIELDS

They sat across a table,
the victorious
and the vanquished,
the men of war.
Their eyes never met.
They read,
they signed,
they saluted
and then departed.
A weary humanity burst
into a celebration of life.
The victims,
all the mothers' sons,
tucked under the killing fields
never heard the cheers.
A lifetime has come and gone
but the killing fields
are still here,
everywhere,
with us,
more deadly,
more vicious,
feeding on fresh blood.
The men of war never go away,
they'll always be here,
in our midst,
forever finding reasons
to kill.
And the violence roars on.
And the pain never ends.

WHAT WILL MAN DO?

Man stands alone
amid a crowd,
steadfast
in the pursuit of life's illusions.
He feeds on the fleeting reality
of what he sees,
as he toils,
blindly
amid questionable choices
and fanciful dreams.
Suddenly,
the night shadows fall,
and Man finds himself
waiting
at the threshold of eternity,
alone,
tired
and bare,
carrying within his heart
a heavy load
of false hopes
and shattered illusions.
What will Man do then?
What will he do?

A REMEMBRANCE OF CHRISTMAS

There were no trees

standing in the room,

trimmed with tinsel

of silver and gold.

There were no lights,

blinking

in many shades of color.

There were no boxes

wrapped with ribbons and tassels.

Beneath a window ledge,

upon a table strewn with hay,

a wooden manger stood,

with Baby Jesus

lying upon a bed of straw.

Mary was on her knees

as Joseph gazed in awe,

amid the shepherds and the sheep.

And I was there,

part of the scene,

watching,

touching,

feeling,

caught up in the mistery.

And I began to cry

for Baby Jesus,

naked and cold,

lying upon a bed of straw.

CHRISTMAS IN MANHATTAN

On a street corner of Manhattan,

a woman sits on the ground.

Nestled in her arms,

a child whimpers in his sleep.

A man staggers by,

waving an empty bottle.

A bell jingles,

as a trumpet blares "Joy to the World"

People come and go

carrying fancy boxes.

Snowflakes dance slowly in the air

as the evening shadows fall.

Store windows glitter

in a choreography of flashing hues.

People rush to catch a train.

A bell keeps jiggling,

and a trumpet keeps blaring,

and the child keeps whimpering in his sleep.

It's Christmas

in the Big Apple.

Joseph Cione

THE HANGING SAGA

They ran,

from sea to shining sea

the Chosen Ones.

They talked and they argued,

they fibbed and they flubbed,

amid the cheering and the jeering,

and also a bit of sneering.

Finally, the ballots were cast,

and the nation waited,

and waited,

and then waited some more.

"There is a roadblock in Florida!"

was the cry the lawyers heard,

and they descended,

by the hundreds,

gleefully,

upon the troubled spot.

Endlessly

they argued,

with silver tongues

and dreams of gold

over deceiving butterflies

and an uncommon breed

of peculiar chads,

some dimpled,

others fully pregnant,

and still others beset by a stubborn streak

that dared to hang.

40

In the end,

out of the Supreme Halls of Justice,

the Voice of Wisdom

spoke the words

that made the Bushes smile

and the Gores groan.

Suddenly,

the crop of dimpled chads

from a swarm of pregnant butterflies

began to wither

in the scorching heat

of the Floridian sun.

REMEMBERING JOAQUIN

(The man I called my son)
It was the noontime of his life,
his smile was warm
and joy lived in his heart.
Manly was his bearing
but gentle were his ways.
His laughter
rang fresh and pure
like water cascading
from the side of a mountain.
One summer day,
death rushed in
to claim him,
and dragged him,
swiftly,
across the rocks,
beneath the bitter waters,
the husband,
the father,
the son,
the friend,
a gift to all who knew him
and loved him.
And the pain never ends.

THE SAGA
OF THE CROOKED NEEDLE

She came inside,

Jill is her name,

smiling,

armed with a crooked needle

and a thread that split into four thinner ones,

each pointing to a different direction.

"Thread the needle!"

she said,

and she smiled once more.

The task was not an easy one.

Nay, it was difficult indeed!

"Give me some wax!"

Sara pleaded, but all came to naught.

Until Elizabeth, a young woman who professed to be blind,

put her two fingers in,

and, voila!

With a patient and steady demeanor

she guided the stubborn thread

through the crooked needle.

Jill finally smiled,

Elizabeth beamed,

and Sara dumped the wax.

I was left wondering:

Why couldn't I do it?

The answer came quickly:

I was only half blind!

HAWKS ARE BIRDS OF PREY

1. It all started on morning on the eleventh of September with terror in Manhattan we will always remember.

2. Bin Laden was the culprit, it was quickly agreed and the hunt was on for Osama and his breed.

3. "I want him at any cost!" was the Chief's mighty sound: "Search every cave!" But, Osama was not found.

4. "No matter!- figured the Chief- we'll get Saddam instead! This creep has got to go. He even tried to kill my dad!"

5. Deaf to world's opinion and bursting at the seam, the Chief launched his attack against Saddam and his regime.

6. Soon, bombs began to fall and rockets began to fly, the innocent began to suffer and thousands had to die.

7. "We come to bring democracy" was the Chief's bold refrain "God is on our side to hell with Saddam Hussein."

8. Eventually the war ended, as they always do, and though Saddam was found, the Chief still needs a clue.

9. With havoc everywhere and looters having fun, the hawks started screeching "Hurray! the war is won!"

10. Meanwhile, the search is on according to the CIA presumption, but no one has yet found weapons of mass destruction.

11. Many weeks have passed since the Chief's proclamation but our soldiers are still dying, in defense of our nation?

12. Nobody knows the future but this is pretty sure: The hawks will keep preying if this Chief will endure.

A DREAM

Riding the morning breeze

upon a ray of sun,

a child,

bright eyed and fair of face,

came to rest over an abyss

deep and wide.

A man, resting on a rock, was staring,

his eyes lost somewhere,

very far.

"Why are you sitting there,

-asked the child-

so glum and sad of eye?

What's your name?"

"My names are many,

-was the reply-

and so are my faces.

I can be all the things I want to be."

"Oh, tell me a few."

Said the child with mischies in his eyes.

The man turned his stare again

far into the distance,

and began to speak:

"I am the wounded remnant of a peculiar breed, exquisitely created out

of love,

destined to live forever.

I am a faithless jumble of living creatures, progeny of evolved apes,

not interested in knowing either the beginning,

or the ending.

45

I am a brimming cauldron simmering with the hopes of many,

forever searching, wanting, choosing

between the ways of justice and peace

and the senseless pursuits of reckless dreams.

I am the voice of evil, echoing in all corners of the world.

I am the face of innocence, once honored,

now, easy prey of vice and greed.

I am a relentless voice clamoring for the right to choose.

I am a voiceless creature smothered within my mother's womb.

I am the face of the poor hungering for justice and the right to live.

I am the heavy arm of power, ready to strike the defenseless and the

meek.

I am an oak tree flaunting my beauty and my strength.

I am a weed, meek and defenseless, struggling to see the sun.

I am a leaf, wrikled and faded, yearning for the cooleness of the summer

rain,

hoping to see, once more, the rising of the new sun.

Mankind is my name.

What's yours?"

"They call me Hope

- was the reply -

I was sent to give you courage

and the will to persevere

to the end.

I make all things new."

And the child left

as he came,

riding the morning breeze

upon a ray of sun.

AND THE PAIN NEVER ENDS

A cloudless sky reveled

in the glow

of the morning sun.

A cool breeze rushed

across the New York bay,

causing ripples upon the surface of the sea.

Life stirred anew everywhere,

announcing the beginning of a new day:

Tuesday, September 11, 2001.

Amid the familiar display

of man's ingenuity and wealth,

the Twin Towers

stood taller and prouder,

gleaming against the rising sun.

Suddenly,

evil most wicked and foul

thrust all its wrath

against the Towers,

with billowing clouds of dust

and tongues of fire.

Wounded and burning,

the Towers crumbled quickly

into a smoldering rubble.

Beneath the clutter and the dust,

thousands of innocent victims

47

shared a common grave.

And the horror,

unspeakable and vile,

will linger

as a haunting memory

that numbs the mind

and wounds the heart.

THE HEROES

They came from everywhere,

the Heroes,

by the hundreds,

with trucks, ladders

and all their familiar gear.

And they rushed,

fearlessly,

into the face of danger,

holding within their hearts

a commitment

and a hope,

as they toiled

tirelessly

amid mountainf of smoldering rubble

and swirling clouds of toxic dust.

The whole world beheld their faces,

stained with soot and grime,

and watched their bodies

boldly thrust

into the jaws of death.

Death came

suddenly,

swiftly,

to still the hearts of many.

But those to whom fate was kinder

49

did not flinch.

They stood their ground

undaunted,

searching tirelessly,

digging

hoping,

praying

that someone,

may live.

THE FIRE KEEPS BURNING

Come friend,

come inside!

It's cold where you are,

and dreary.

From the mountains

and across the valleys,

a foul wind howls

a sickening tune.

Come friend,

come inside!

where the cold no longer stings

and the howling is heard no more.

Upon the hearth

a never ending fire glows,

and the beckoning flames

shed comfort and light

to all who seek them,

to all who need them.

Come friend,

come inside!

The night shadows

are falling,

amid the frigid cold

and the fury of the wind.

Come, friend!

51

The door is never locked,

and the fire keeps burning

for you,

for me,

and for all God's children,

forevermore.

A NEW DAWN

A faint light
slowly rises above the mountains,
chasing away the darkness
across the sky.
A bird's choir
welcomes the rising sun
with melodies learned long ago.
It's the dawn of a new day,
another day,
offered,
as a gift,
to urge us
to love one another
with words yet unspoken
and deeds yet undone;
to hope,
to dream
for a world that never was,
where a child can lead a tiger
to a running stream
and show no fear;
where men have no swords to sharpen,
but a hand to offer,
always,
as a covenant
of lasting peace.

SIC TRANSIT GLORIA...

On top of a hill,

wrapped in the glow of the autumn sun,

a maple tree

flaunts his festive garb

in warm hues

fluttering in the wind.

But fleeting is the splendor,

and brief the acclaim.

Soon, the leaves will fall,

one by one,

wrinkled and faded,

useless debris,

shuffled by the wind.

And the tree will stand,

naked and lonely,

on top of a hill,

easy prey of winter's wrath.

Only within its core,

the spark of life will still be there,

undiminished,

holding the promise

of a new spring.

YEARNING FOR SPRING

I've had enough
of winter's anger,
mounts of snow and freezing rain,
I 've had enough with gloom and pain.
I've had enough of murky skies
and foul weather gear,
I've had enough already
enough to shed a tear.
I long to see the sky
with birds on the wing,
I long to welcome April
bearing the first kiss of spring.

WE ALL NEED A FRIEND

When in your life
an ill wind blows,
causing pain
and lots of woes,
listen to your heart,
stretch out a hand,
you need a friend.
When the clouds get dark and heavy
and life is on the wane,
causing strife
and added pain,
listen to your heart,
sretch out a hand,
you need a friend.
And when you finally see the rainbow
shining clear and bright,
causing your mind to see
a glimmer of the guiding light,
listen to your heart,
start listening to the Word,
you need the Lord!

AN ODE TO SARA

God chose you, and fashioned you

preciously,

within your mother's womb.

As a wife

and a mother,

out of you, life sprung forth six times,

six new hearts

and souls

destined to live forever.

God took you by the hand,

and taught you how to be

a comforter,

a nurturer,

and a healer.

Amid the joys and the pain,

the laughter and the tears,

the children grew,

and in you they found

a teacher,

a counselor

and a friend.

From you,

they learned to love, to hope, to trust and to forgive.

After a lifetime,

deep from within your heart,

faith shines forth like a burst of dawn,

and within your soul,

love lives

as warm and as radiant

as the noonday sun.

And your name is Sara.

A DREAM FULFILLED

It was the early morning hours
of a day of spring.
Snowflakes were dancing
in the chilly air,
like confetti
scattered
as a sign of welcome,
just for me.
Amid the snow and the fog,
I felt the heart of America,
throbbing
in unison with mine,
amid the countless diaphanous lights
flickering,
all around,
assuring me that I was finally home.
An arm raised high
holding a torch
with a light,
shining
through the fog and the snowflakes,
echoed within my mind
the sound of words I had heard before,
long ago,
on my father's knees:
"This is the place to be, my son!
America is the place, where freedom reigns
and hope never dies."

REVERIE

Now,
a lifetime later,
here I am,
watching the setting sun,
as memories rush in,
crowding the mind
with warm gleams of long ago:
Trails I explored,
hills I climbed,
plains I wandered through,
Under a murky sky
or kissed by a blazing sun:
glowing faces,
chuckling voices
of those I love,
blessings of a lifetime
are these,
precious and timeless,
gifts
from a loving God,
whose merciful hand
is still reaching for mine,
as I bask,
unworthily,
in the mercy of His Love.

~ SELECTED ESSAYS ~

THE ARRIVAL

It was Wednesday morning of March 26, 1947. The booming voice of Captain Blough was heard loud and clear through the ship's loudspeakers. It had a cheerful ring to it: *"Buon giorno! Tempesta finita! Fa bel tempo! Domani, Nuova York! Domani, America! Si, si America!"*

He repeated the message several times, pronouncing each word slowly, to make sure that we understood him. He was aware of his limited knowledge of Italian, nevertheless, he made a valiant effort to communicate with us the best he could. He wanted us to know that, finally, the storm had passed, the weather was good and that the following day we would be arriving to New York, to America, and that the atmospheric nightmare we had endured for fifteen days was finally over.

Captain Blough, a giant of a man, powerfully built and gifted with an easy smile and a friendly attitude, was the skipper of the "Marine Park", a so-called Victory ship built during World War II and used to transport American troops and supplies to the European front.

The "Shark" had left the harbor of Palermo, Sicily, on the 12 of March with about one hundred emigrants, mostly Sicilians and a few others from the neighboring Calabria. Women and children of school age made up for the bulk of the passengers. There was also a small number of elderly people as well as young people in their twenties. My mother and I were among them. I was 21 years old and my mother had just completed her 55th birthday.

During the interminable journey, two back-to-back storms raged for days in the middle of the Atlantic Ocean, testing the skill, the courage and the stamina of Capt. Blough and his crew, as well as the patience and the spirit of all of us, the passengers, particularly the young ones.

During those frightening hours, the ship was at the mercy of the elements, as it rose and dipped continuously like a wooden horse on a merry-go-around. Like a prizefighter caught on the ropes, the "Shark" did all it could to come out of it unscathed. And it did, with a lot of creaking and groaning, but unharmed and undaunted.

Deep down its bowels, many people, scared to death, managed to huddle together, some crying, others praying. My mother, rosary beads at hand, prayed the loudest, urging the rest of us to do the same.

As it often happens in the course of our lives, eventually the sunshine will break through the dark clouds to bring us courage and hope. Capt. Blough's announcement was just that. His words were meant to give us courage and hope.

Often times, I think about that morning, the captain's voice, his kind attitude, his compassion and the jubilant way with which we welcomed his announcement. Most of us still in our pajamas, let go with joyful shouts as if we had just been unshackled and freed from a long and cruel torture.

As the sun was about to rise above the horizon, Capt. Blough invited all those who wished, except the children, to join him on the deck to watch nature's most dramatic event. Many accepted the invitation, wrapped in blankets to brave the chilly breeze.

The sky was clear and the sea was calm, a rare sight indeed for all of us. Frothy wawes kept chasing one another across the boundless sea. They had finally dissipated their anger, and the wind had checked its fury and turned it into a cool and pleasant breeze.

We all gathered near the captain, leaning against the railings. We trained our eyes toward tho horizon and waited. Soon, the blackness of the sky changed into a shade of blue. No one said a word. I had the feeling that we were participating in a religious ceremony.

Meanwhile, the sky kept changing its color. At the horizon line, we watched orange, yellow and pink hues coming together, in a continuous flow, creating a canvass of unmatchable beauty.

Finally, within seconds, the upper rim of the sun rose above the horizon, creating a brilliant crown that lit the sky. It seemed as if the sea was giving birth to the sun. Across its surface, a shimmering, silvery streak appeared as to celebrate the event.

As dawn broke, the sun kept rising and the silvery streak turned into a sparkling sheath all around.

A few minutes after, we followed the captain to the mess hall, where we ate a quick breakfast and walked right out. We all had a lot of packing to do, getting our immigration papers and passports ready for inspection and also getting ready, mentally and emotionally, to meet the members of our families, who made it possible for all of us to come to America.

Before I went to bed, I climbed to the main deck to check the weather conditions. What I saw caused me to panic. Dark clouds were gathering at the horizon, and a strong breeze was beginning to stir things around. Could it be that another storm was beginning to brood somewhere ahead of us?

Toward midnight, the voice of the captain came through the loudspeakers, this time in a softer tone, almost a whisper: *"Arriviamo a Nuova York, solo due ore!"* We'll arrive in New York in two hours, he said.

After the announcement, all one hundred of us were in a state of continuous flux. We all wanted to go up on deck to enjoy every exciting moment of the event unfolding before our eyes. We wanted to watch the fable turn into reality, the fascinating fable about the New World that we heard and read about so much.

Two hours passed quickly. Capt. Blough gave us permission to stay on the deck. The temperature was near freezing, and we could see snowflakes dancing in the breeze. For us Sicilians, snow and freezing temperatures were two unknown phenomena.

At about 2:00 AM of March 27, 1947, the "Marine Shark" finally reached New York Bay area. In spite of the darkness, countless flickering lights came to view. They looked like votive candles lit up to honor the event. A roar rose from the crowd.

The ship kept inching its way into the docking peer. At 2:30, the "Shark" came to a stop. The anchors were lowered and the engines stopped humming. The long journey was finally over. It took 15 days, 14 nights and 9 hours.

The snow continued to dance in the air. A thin layer was beginning to appear on the floor of the deck. We all extended our hands trying to catch the snowflakes as if they were butterflies. I waited 21 years, 5 months and 4 days to make a snowball, marvel at it and bite into it as if it were a sun-ripened Sicilian orange.

It was bitter cold, at least for us Sicilians, but not many of us would let the cold steal from us the unique opportunity to watch the awesome spectacle that lay before our eyes.

Besides the atmospheric show that continued undisturbed, we saw huge structures shrouded in fog and seemingly reaching for the sky. Out of them, thousands of lights shimmered like stars on a dark night, lending the scene an aura of mystery, a sight strange and alluring at the same time.

At one point, Capt. Blough gathered us around him, pointed a finger toward the area where the Staue of Liberty was located, but because of the bad weather conditions, we were unable to discern the familiar shape of the world-famous landmark. We could barely see the light atop the torch.

At the urgings of the captain, we all went below deck and to our bunks to catch a few hours of sleep.

The next morning, we all joined him and his crew for our last breakfast aboard the "Shark"He was in a bubbly mood. We took the opportunity to show him our gratitude for his great skill, courage and friendly attitude that he showed throughout the trip.

Then came the time to say goodbye. Around 9: 00 AM, Captain Blough and his crew gathered at the exiting gate. We shook hands, some wiped away tears and some children ended up in the arms of the captain and the crew.

As I first stepped on the American soil, on my way to the inspection proceedings, I kept thinking of Capt. Blough. He was only one man, only one voice, but I saw in him all the skill, all the generosity and all the compassion of America. In his voice, I heard the voice of all Americans saying to me: "Welcome! Welcome to America!"

Joseph Cione

THE AMERICAN FLAG
IS <u>NOT</u>
FOR BURNING

We, Americans, have been hearing for quite a while the shrill voices of some pseudo- intellectuals, whose pretentious rhetoric is an affront to all the citizens of this great country.

It seems that those self-appointed guardians of our constitutional freedom have somehow come up with the notion that unless we, Americans, are forbidden the "right" to burn our flag, "The Old Glory", "The Stars and Stripes", we are not totally free!

Of course, they say, there must be a good reason for it. And the "good" reason they came up with is "as an act of legitimate protest" against the government of the United States.

Another conclusion that the liberal minds have arrived at is that the flag, per se, is only an abstraction, a mere piece of cloth sewn together in a particular pattern. What's all the commotion about? They ask.

In America, where democracy lives, we have had a long history of showing our grievances in every imaginable public arena. We use picketing, strikes, random acts of civil disobedience, writing campaigns to our elected officials, and if nothing works, we can seek justice in a court of law. When, then, does the burning of our flag become a more efficient way to express complaints or regress injustices?

As for the flag being "only an abstraction", I would like to see someone who feels that way to get enough courage to appear in one of the American Veteran Organizations meetings, on the Fourth of July, in any American city, and try to convince anyone in uniform that the flag is only "an abstraction", just a piece of cloth sewn together, no big deal!

The idea of burning the flag and the assent given by the U.S. Supreme Court in 1989, constitute an affront to the millions of American service men and women, who fought valiantly overseas, and for whom the American flag was and still is a "concrete"symbol of the United States of America, its heritage, its freedom, and its way of life.

In the summer of 1943, I lived in Sicily, as a young teenager, and I witnessed the invasion of the island by the American forces. In the small town I was living at the time, a small group of American soldiers on jeeps drove through the main road. They stopped for a while, investigated the peaceful countryside, and, in the end, five of them remained. They quickly installed telephone lines on the existing poles and made themselves comfortable by erecting a huge tent in the middle of someone's wheat field.

As an Italian and as a member of the Fascist Youth Organization, they were my enemies, and I had been warned not to fraternize with them.

The house I was staying at was located just across the road from them. I was watching them every day. They seemed to be always in good humor. They did their assigned chores and then they relaxed playing catch or singing or playing a guitar. They all seemed to be on a picnic instead of a war.

One morning, I witnessed a remarkable event. It impressed me so much that I still remember it very vividly, sixty-one years later.

The one, who appeared to be the leader, came out of the tent holding a bundle between his arms and his chest. Four soldiers followed him in a military fashion. They stopped in front of a pole that they had erected next to one corner of the tent. As the leader unfolded the bundle and attached it to the rope that was hanging from the pole, I recognized the American flag.

As the flag was being pulled up slowly, the four soldiers, smartly lined up, stood to attention and saluted until the flag reached the top of the pole. After the salute, the leader shouted something and the five of them marched off smartly into the tent.

I saw all that from a distance, and what they did and how they did affect me a great deal. The short event spoke volumes about the way that the Americans felt, and still feel, about their country, their love for it and their pride in their way of life.

After that occasion, I became their friend and they became my friends. The name of the sergeant was Erwing Metting, and he was from Texas.

In a popular photo taken at Iwo Jima, in the Pacific war front, during World War II, four Marines are seen in the process of raising the "Old Glory" on one of the island's post. The photo clearly shows what the flag meant to them.

Sixty years later, let's not start demeaning their courage, belittling their sacrifice and insulting their patriotism. No, the American flag is not for burning!

IN GOD WE TRUST

It is a fundamental principle in the American history that this land, this unique, rich and generous nation was created in the belief that Almighty God is the only source of all that is good, all that is free and all that is just.

It is also an irrefutable truth, too often overlooked, that our Founding Fathers were remarkable men endowed with wisdom and religious faith.

This explicit dependence on divine providence is clearly mentioned in the Declaration of Independence: *"All men are created equal, that they are endowed by their Creator with certain unalienable rights."* in the fourth stanza of the National Anthem: *"and this is our motto: In God we trust!"* and in the Pledge of Allegiance: *"one nation under God, indivisible, with liberty and justice for all!"*

"In God We Trust" has been imprinted in our currency since 1864, as a reminder of our relationship with our Creator.

In the past century, millions of people from many parts of the world, my family included, have left their birthplaces, and crossed the oceans to set foot in the *"Promised Land"* holding within their hearts the fervent hope to share in the *American Dream.*

Soon they discovered that as they worked, persevered and kept their trust in God, the *American Dream* was not an empty promise; it became indeed a tangible reality. The welcoming words sculpted on the base of the Statue of Liberty in New York's harbor were not just words to be read and soon forgotten; they were and still are the true essence of America, a nation wrought in generosity and compassion.

It is my belief that it is because of such qualities that the Lord has continued to bless America and its people.

At the dawn of the new millennium, we, Americans, live in a society thoroughly caught up in the crosswinds of a technological revolution.

During the past half a century, the last decade in particular, the creative power of the human brain has been hard at work to create a world mostly dependent on the speed and accuracy of amazing electronic machines. If the trend continues, as it seems that it will, a time may come when the motto *"In God We Trust"* will be deprived of its importance and even its meaning, thus becoming just an historical quotation.

What we are witnessing today is the perennial battle between two powerful forces, Matter and Spirit, and the outcome will ultimately decide the destiny of the human race.

With society more and more enticed by the allurements of the material accomplishments, it seems that any suggestion that the future of mankind is still dependent on the will of God is out of step with life's realities, and therefore, it might sound incongruous and unacceptable.

One factor that strongly militates against peoples' acceptance of the spiritual concept of divine dependence is the tendency to believe that they are self-sufficient and capable of deciding the road to follow, on their own. In the course of one's life, the relentless pursuit of wealth, fame and power automatically excludes the necessity to rely on the providence of God.

In the final analysis, it seems that it has been already decided that only *"the meek shall possess the earth"* (Mt. 5:5) and not the wealthy, the famous and the powerful.

A survey of today's life priorities shared by the so-called entertainment media puts into focus some of the reasons that contribute to the spiritual alienation that affects the present society.

There is little doubt that what's being shown in the tabloids, in the movies and TV screens, whether subtly or blatantly, contributes a great deal to the creation of moods, perceptions and attitudes that the viewers, especially the weak-willed and the adolescents, tend to absorb and make their own

All that is written, said and shown in most of the media's daily programs have the necessary allure and the power to influence and eventually re-arrange the life's priorities of those who read, hear or watch them.

Often times, the result is that people's understanding of right and wrong, truth and lie, virtue and wickedness becomes so blurred that the distinction between the extremes is no longer perceived. As result, the right to achieve the "want" is preferred to the moral responsibility to insure the "ought"

Here is a question that begs for an answer: Why should any member of our society, who is absorbed in his/her own accomplishments and is satisfied with what he/she is reaping from life, have anything to do with God, whose requirements include moral restrictions and obedience?

It is probably true that the so-called self-made people would shy away from any form of restriction in their pursuit of material perfection. Therefore, it is probable that such people would rather continue worshipping the gods, who require neither moral restrictions nor spiritual affiliation. The false gods liable to be pursued could be numerous and varied, like Wealth, Power, Fame, Sex, Physical Beauty, Eternal Youth, etc.

Ultimately, life boils down to making choices. God Almighty, in His infinite wisdom, has given a great gift to all his creatures: free will. He is not interested in pulling our strings, like a puppet master. He gave us perfect directions to follow, as we continue to wander in our individual journeys toward our eternal destiny.

As the battle between Good and Evil is being fought on the planet Earth, it is imperative for each one of us, who are on the side of Good, that we accept God's plans, that we let Him know that He is in charge of our lives, and that we accept His sovereignty until we draw our last breath.

Let *"In God We Trust"* be our battle cry, as it was in the hearts and lips of our ancestors. Let it be for us a constant reminder that we are God's

Joseph Cione

creatures, and we must love Him, obey Him and serve Him continually and unreservedly.

Ultimately, *"In God We Trust"* means that we trust His Wisdom, we feel secure in His Will and we feel safe in His Mercy.

A SHORT MOUSE TALE

For sometime, I was able to resist the temptation to join the rest of the human race and become a computer addict.

I had been listening to friends and family members sing out lavish praises with passion and awe, and in order for me to resist their continuous urgings, I had to summon all the stubborn energy at my disposal. I had reached the point when I felt guilt-ridden just for not owning the darn thing.

"How can you function in today's world without the help of a computer?"

This was the accusation that I kept reading in their eyes, and because of it, I was beginning to develop a complex of some kind that made me feel ill at ease.

I tried in many way to defend, or at least explain, the reason for my reluctance to join the computer bandwagon. The more efforts I made, the more I realized that all of them were only poor attempts to camouflage the truth.

And here was the crux of the matter: I felt intimidated by computers. Honest! I couldn't even explain it to myself, but every time I glanced on one of them, I experienced an anxiety attack.

When I was inside an electronic store and walked from aisle to aisle, I <u>knew</u> that they were there, somewhere, sneering at me with an air of insolent superiority. And they weren't even turned on!

I swear, often times, I felt like going after them, stick out my tongue at them or even put my fist through their hideous glass eye and laugh at them.

Joseph Cione

Fortunately, my reason triumphed over my impulse and I managed to walk away from them. Besides, I didn't want to create a scene.

Well, one day, it just happened that a local newspaper ran a full-page advertisement about a certain make of computers that were on sale for much less that I had previously seen. My knees began to buckle and the heart began to flutter. Could it be? Yes, indeed, I found myself caught up in the whirlwind of a disgraceful surrender, the beginning of a shameful compromise with my principles.

I immediately summoned my son-in-law Bob, who was a self-taught whiz on computers, received his expert opinion, and before I had time to recuperate from the shock, we were at the Store, inspecting the merchandise.

With Bob doing all the necessary inspection of the computer on sale and asking all the questions concerning its quality and capabilities, I kept a low profile, still trying to find in my mind a plausible reason for my shameful surrender.

Having completed the purchase of the various components, Bob and I walked out of the store with a complete computer, a printer and a scanner. As I was ready to drive off, Bob said matter-of-factly: "Congratulations, dad! You are now a member of the computer generation. Your life will never be the same." That wasn't exactly what I wanted to hear.

At home, Bob put everything together for me, ready to come to life at the push of a button. He explained to me all that I could absorb on the first lesson. He went home reassuring me that my life will change for the better.

Before I pushed the first button, I stood in front of the computer; I stared into its blank expression and, suddenly, a nagging thought popped into my head:

What if this silicon-brained know-it-all, fully aware of the limited capabilities of my brain, decided on its own, and in full view of my friends and family members, to fill the screen with something like "Aren't you too stupid to play with my mouse? Are you sure that you are ready to treat me with all the respect that I deserve?"

Yeah, the idea of putting my fist through the arrogant glass eye came up again to challenge my patience. This time the thought was quickly dismissed for economic reasons.

As the weeks went by, Bob kept spoon-feeding me electronic mush. During that time, I tried to be acquainted with the mouse by clicking the stuffing out of it. Sometimes, it got even with me by disappearing when I needed it the most. Other times, on spite I am sure, it kept pointing to the wrong items.

As I kept pushing the keys, clicked the stubborn mouse, tried to follow the instructions, tried to decipher the hieroglyphics on the bars, my frustration began to mount. Apparently pushing one key instead of another was enough of a blunder to cause a perfectly sane individual to be transformed into a raving lunatic.

One suggestion that I received from many sources was to take advantage of the HELP sign shown on the menu bar, but more often than not, the advice offered had nothing to do with the problem I was facing. In fact, the hideous looking paperclip seemed to be sneering at me, seemingly rejoicing in my failures.

One day, more frustrated than ever, I decided to buy a simple computer primer that would speak to me with a much simpler tone than the one used in the instruction booklet that came with the purchase. I swallowed my pride and decided to buy a book entitled: WORD'97 FOR DUMMIES.

The book was entertaining, written with humor, and it had lots of tips and shortcuts. However, when it came to regular cuts, the electronic fog descended upon me thick, dark and impenetrable.

I decided that I needed something easier than that.

The following day, I went back to the store, where a young woman welcomed me with a smile. I showed her the title of the book and asked her if she could suggest an easier one. "Is there anything wrong with the book you have?" She asked. "This book is for dummies." I replied in a whisper. "Do you happen to have one for Complete Idiots?"

Her face broke into a wide grin, unsure whether I was serious or was I speaking in jest. Then, she offered a bit of her humor, saying: "Sorry, Sir, the book you have has the lowest IQ of all the books in the store." She looked at me, and smiled again.

I smiled back sheepishly and walked out of the store, holding under my arm the source of my embarrassment.

A few years have passed since those frustrating and embarrassing days. Now, my computer and I are friends. Well, I don't mean that we are pals yet, because sometimes my friend still shows a penchant for arrogant behavior, which I counter with my own kind of disrespectful demeanor. In total, however, we have reached a point of reciprocal understanding and respect.

Today, I see my computer as an awesome wizard, unpredictable and capricious still, but a very helpful friend, indeed. It keeps opening doors for me into the exciting world of the unknown, where I dare to navigate, timidly still, across this seemingly endless ocean of possibilities. Most of the fog has dispelled and streams of light are now shining through. Even the mouse has decided to become my friend. I don't abuse it anymore. As matter of fact, when I click it, I do it gently now, almost apologetically. I don't want to hurt its feelings, anymore.

Joseph Cione

CHRISTMAS IN SICILY

(A remembrance)

The period to which I refer includes the pre- world war years, particularly the decade of the thirties, when life was simple and the people lived it, one day at a time, in joyful harmony among themselves and with genuine faith in their God.

This is a remembrance of my childhood, in the village of Gioiosa Marea, where I was born. It's a remembrance of Christmas, the preparation, the celebration, the meaning of it all.

Christmas celebration generally began around the middle of December, at the end of the fishing season. The entire village community became alive with joyous excitement, affecting young and old, rich and poor.

It was, above all, a religious feast, a Holy Day in the strictest sense of the word. It was a time for sharing, a time for rejoicing and a time for praying. It was more of a community celebration that it was a family celebration.

In those days, Santa was unknown as it was television and its commercial hype. It was unimaginable that the meaning and solemnity of Christmas could be trivialized by thought or deed.

There were no trees to decorate or shopping sprees to fret about. No one expected to receive any gift-wrapped in fancy paper or any other kind of paper, not even the children.

We expected to receive a gift on January 6, the Feats of the Epiphany. According to an ancient legend, vaguely based on biblical references, the Magi Kings on their return voyage from Bethlehem would pass by the house of the "good" children and reward them with gifts. For that day, there were no "bad" children in the community.

The traditional ritual was that every child would have to leave a shoe outside one of the window ledges filled with straw, which was intended for the Magi camels, presumably tired and hungry after the long trip.

On the early morning of the seventh we would rush to the designated window to retrieve our gifts, which generally consisted of bags of hazel nuts, hard candy, chocolate bars, rubber balls, etc. The rich boys might find a soccer ball and the girls a raggedy doll. Of course, the straw had disappeared from the shoe, proof certain for us that the camels had indeed passed by our windows.

Christmas preparations began with a thorough cleaning of the house. This was the time of the year when all the people of the village would follow an old tradition according to which they would go visiting at least seven households, visit the nativity scene called "Presepio" pray over it and exchange home-made cookies called "cucciddati," a Sicilian specialty, filled with a mixture of dry figs, honey and nuts.

The "Presepio" was another respected Sicilian tradition. It was a large representation of the nativity scene, usually built on one corner of the living room. The base was made out of wood and on top of it, using a great deal of papier-mache, mountains, rivers, houses and caves were fashioned to simulate a village like Bethlehem. The main part of this construction, of course, was the Stable were most of the attention was focused. The last thing to do was to place the traditional figurines on the proper places.

A week before Christmas, shepherds from the nearby hills took time off from their flock to come to our village and other villages close by. They were dressed in their natural winter attire made of sheepskin from head to toe. The tradition was to stop in front of the houses where they had been invited, and play Christmas Carols on their bagpipes. For their effort, they received "cucciddati," dry figs, nuts or a bottle of homemade wine, which they collected into sacks made also of sheepskin.

Christmas Eve was observed also according to the ongoing tradition, which dictated that at least three kinds of fish should be served, and one of them should be "baccarat'" (dry, salty codfish cooked with tomato sauce, black olives and capers.)

79

That night, the whole house would be filled with the pungent aroma of the fish, which pleased some, but displeased many others, especially the children, who refused to eat "stinky food."

Another tradition worthy of note was the playing of "tombola" after the meal. It was a family game very similar to the modern "bingo" We used dry beans for chips and the winnings were redeemed with hazel nuts, very abundant in the area.

On Christmas morning, after breakfast, served with "cucciddati" and the usual caffe-latte" (the modern cappuccino), we dressed up with our finest attire and, all together, would walk to San Nicola Church, which was appropriately decorated. An enormous Presepio was displayed on one side of the church interior. The altar was covered with new linen in the traditional colors of red and green. During the celebration of the Mass, the choir would sing several carols, joined by the rest of the congregation.

Finally, the Christmas dinner was prepared and consumed at least by two families, either family members or neighbors. The families would gather at the larger house and share the various traditional dishes, mostly chicken and lamb, cooked in a variety of ways, served with choices of fresh vegetables. Homemade wine was the most popular drink for the grown-ups, while the children drank lemonade and orangeade.

In Gioiosa, like in any other place, there were needy families that had nothing to share, and elderly folks who lived alone. Such families were always included in the festive plans of neighboring families that took turns each year in taking care of them in all their needs. Christmas was a time when no one ate alone. It was a Holy Day, a time to share, a time to rejoice in, and, most of all, a time to love one another, as the Lord God urges us to do, every day of our lives.

THE CONFERENCE

The youngest of my children is a Research Scientist, who works for an agency of the U.S. Government called N.O.A.A. (National Oceanographic and Atmospheric Agency). He deals with the atmospheric part of it. He researches hurricanes, and to find out more about their behavior, he and some of his colleagues, from time to time, fly through the "eye" of some of them to make a number of tests, measurements, etc.

These guys live dangerously, but they love the adventure and appreciate the challenge. What they do also is writing reports about all the tests they take and all the experiments they perform. I read some of them, and, believe me, these fellows know their stuff. I assume that they do, anyway. Considering the words that they use, I figure that they must be very smart. They must be in order to understand themselves when they speak about their projects.

Once, I asked my son if the kind of English they use in all their writings could be actually a codified language, invented by the C.I.A. during the cold-war period, for the purpose of confusing the minds of the Soviet meteorological experts, and prevent them from taking advantage of the weather for a sneaky attack on the American shores. Too far fetched? Maybe.

Listen to the words that I took out of my son's thesis: Frontogenesis, geopotential height, coastal cyclogenesis, cold advection, horizontal baroclinicity, mesocyclone, etc.

Did you know that "All vertical diffusion terms are computed via a time-implicit scheme that allows the model to use a time step which is not constrained by vertical diffusion?" To tell the truth, I didn't know this. Do you still think that my hypothesis is too far fetched? Think again!

Anyway, let me tell you about the conference I attended a few years ago at the Mesolow Center in Vortex, N.Y. The main point of the conference was to discuss the causes as well as the unusual developments of the so-called Storm of the Century, which played havoc in the entire eastern coastline of the United States in the year 1999.

To assure the success of the conference, several personalities in the world of meteorology were invited to speak, among them: Dr. Adia Batic, head of the Weattle Weather Bureau in Oregon, Prof. A. Kuechistu, from Ankara National University in Turkey, Dr. J. Awaddira, Director of the Baroclinicity Institute in Beirut and Dr. I.M. Cosidipazzi , Inspector General of the National Meteorological Systems of the Region of Sicily, and Professor Emeritus of the "Instituto Meteorologico dell'Universita` Tiravento" in the city of Catania.

Dr. Adia Batic, who was also the Mistress of Ceremony, introduced Dr. Kuechistu as the first speaker. In spite of his pronounced accent, the illustrious guest spoke clearly and cogently and the appreciative audience, among whom there was a sizable contingent of graduate students from the various universities of the try-state area, welcomed him with a rousing applause.

His triumphal moment came when he made the following statement:

"The unusual power and length of the storm was largely due to the high diffusity of the moist convection, which caused a serious frontolitic impact to adversely advect the influence field already parametized by the latent heat influx, which had its origin in the Gulf of Mexico."

Dr. Awaddira was introduced as the second speaker. He spoke with a thick accent also, but without the peculiar inflexion that we heard previously from Dr. Kuechistu.

His remarks were received with shouts of approval and thunderous applause. Here is the most important point the made:

"With all due respect, I beg to differ with some of the conclusions drawn by the learned scientist and friend Dr. Kuechistu. Let me explain. If his conclusions were correct, shouldn't we have seen a sizable increase in the quasi-symmetric low-level vortex as well as a decrease in the adiabatic lapse rate? Was this the case? I don't think so. In fact, the frontolic impact was totally non-existent during the entire cold advective period. Therefore, I believe that the storm acquired its enormous power in the vicinity of Mount Saint Laurel in Maryland, where the thermal gradients parametized by the moisture fluxes, could not distabilize enough to affect the atmospheric static stability." At the end of his talk, he received a standing ovation.

The last speaker was Dr. I.M. Cosidipazzi. As he walked toward the rostrum, with his well-known swaggering gate, a hush filled the amphitheatre. Because of his enormous reputation in the field of meteorology, the feeling of anticipation could be felt in every seat. Then, he began to speak:

"Ladies and gentlemen, let me say first that I disagree with the conclusions reached by my esteemed colleagues. All the reasoning that I have listened to, does not, in my professional estimation, amount to a hill of beans. Let me explain: Tell me, during this so-called Storm of the Century, did the diabatic forcing propagate one single degree above the adiabatic lapse rate? Of course not! And what can we say about the diffusity and the interpolation experienced at the O"Hara Airport in Chicago during the latent heat flux, ah? Did it happen? Of course not! There you have, ladies and gentlemen. The storm was a fake! It was only a simulated mesocyclogenesis. It was a meteorological fraud to confound the untrained eye and mind."

At this point, Dr. Cosidipazzi paused and mopped hi brow, dripping with perspiration. The silence was broken by a voice coming from the back seats of the amphitheatre. It was a student. He said: "What about the snowdrifts in front of my house, six feet high. The snow looked real to me; it was white... cold... wet!" Another student stood up and added: "What about the wind that blew the roof off my garage, ah? It sounded like wind to me!" And another student stood up and said:

"And what about the floods, Dr. Cosidipazzi, what about them? Were they fake too, ah? My car must be floating in the Hudson River by now!"

At this point, Dr. Cosidipazzi's complexion turned into a sickly gray; he put aside his professional composure, and with his arms in a continuous motion, he gave to all those in the audience a genuine demonstration of his emotional Mediterranean ancestry. Dr. Cosidipazzi glared at the gutsy intruders, pointed a finger at them and said:

"You sniveling, quasi-convected low level vortexes, miserable paramitized human deformations, too inexperienced yet to make even a frontolic impact on anything, how dare you challenge my conclusions?

At that point, with the audience aroused by the remarks of the students and by the anger of the response, Dr. Adia Batic decided to declare the conference closed.

Within a short time, the amphitheatre was empty. Outside the arena, Prof. Kuechistu and Dr. Awaddira were treated to enthusiastic applause and shouts of appreciation. Dr. Cosidipazzi, on the other hand, had to deal with several parametized human deformations, who found it proper to launch to the direction of the Professor Emeritus several simulated snowballs which made a frontolic impact around the low level vortexes, without causing any diabatic forcings at all.

Thank God for that!

WHAT WAS THAT, AGAIN?

Has anyone noticed that in recent years, most of the ads on TV, in an attempt to appear sophisticated, have become so convoluted and garbled in style and content that when they leave the screen, the viewer is left wondering what was it all about?

Oftentimes, I find it difficult to sit through many of them because I fail to grasp the hidden meaning of what's being shown. My patience is unfairly tested when the conscious level of my mind is suddenly confronted by a visual sequence that seems to be totally irrelevant to the product being advertised.

I remember the happy years when a straightforward approach, coupled with discernible language used to be the hallmark of every successful business. Today, often enough, I am left baffled, bewildered and bemused by these peculiar marketing techniques that seem to go beyond the acceptable boundaries of entertainment or even plain common sense.

During my younger years, the advertising agencies did not waste any time pussyfooting around esoteric ideas and techniques. No, they went straight to the point, and the meaning was always clear. They appealed to the conscious mind. What we saw on the screen was exactly what we got.

Today's society, thoroughly overwhelmed by this forever changing barrage of sophisticated lifestyles and attitudes, requires, I am told, new and more exciting stimuli, fresher ideas and avant-garde approaches. Madison Avenue found the answer: Subliminal impulses.

My dictionary's definition of "subliminal" is inadequate to produce a conscious awareness. In other words, in order to show interest in a particular product, the viewer's mind must not be in a state of conscious awareness. What they are trying to say to you and me is that in order to appreciate what the ad says, you and I must be in a state of unconsciousness. Do they mean drunk, soused, pickled, and bombed?

Sometime ago, General Motors came up with an ad showing a new truck being driven up a desolate mountain side, over huge boulders, through streams and other rough terrain. As the vehicle kept bouncing, a male voice in the background kept repeating in a raspy tone: "Like a rock! Oh, like a rock!" The truck ended up at the very edge of a cliff, with birds of prey hovering close by.

What I would like to know is, why a vehicle of that kind, obviously built for normal business use, and therefore destined to be used on paved roads is shown climbing a mountain side, parked next to the abyss within a scenario of impending doom? To show that it is tough? What about paved roads; how is the truck on paved roads? And furthermore, what's like a rock, the truck? Is it smart to compare an expensive truck to a rock? A rock does not go anywhere. It does not climb mountains. It falls <u>off</u> mountains!

During the same period, a different auto manufacturer offered another gem of avante- garde ingenuity. It didn't last too long, though. A sleek red jeep was driven into a desolate place. A huge bull kept charging the moving vehicle to no avail. Suddenly, the jeep drove into a slime ditch, disappearing from sight. As it came out, oozing muck, it stopped right in front of a grunting pig. Not a word was spoken about the jeep, or about the whereabouts of the bull.

Since the conscious side of my brain refused to be involved, the sub-conscious side came up with the following hypothesis: If one potential customer was contemplating moving to Pamplona, Spain, he/she would not have any problem enjoying the car there because of the abundant availability of bulls in that region. On the other hand, if he/she preferred to stay in the U.S. and decided to raise a family on a pig farm, the same car would do very well there too. A car wash in the vicinity would be helpful in the end.

Those who still remember the beer "commercials" (remember the word?) of yesteryear, the names Ballantine, Rheingold and Schafer, above all, must evoke a bit of nostalgia. Each of them had a distinct jingle to remind us of baseball and the coming of a new spring.

The commercials were slices of real life. It showed muscular men with tattoos all over their arms, rejoicing in a tavern, guzzling beer out of huge mugs, smacking their lips and wiping them off with the side of their sleeves.

Nowadays, beer ads don't need jingles or tough guys opening beer cans with their teeth. They need new stimuli, like frogs and lizards, clever little devils, which don't haggle over salary and don't need a union card, either. Remember them a few years ago? The Budweiser intelligentsia figured that the subliminal trick would work easily with the beer. Just a look at those two slimy creatures of the marsh world was enough to rekindle in anyone the sensation of thirst, and a trip to the fridge was an automatic exercise. Clever, isn't? But what about the quality of the brew. Was it necessary to inquire about? Naah! The subconscious part of the brain does not waste any time about silly things like that.

The jeans manufacturers of the world know what a brilliant idea it was to elevate the jeans from their lowly role of fatigue gear to the status of elegant garb that they enjoy today.

There are fortunes to be made selling jeans, especially if a well-known designer puts his name on the labels.

Regardless of who the manufacturer is, however, the ads shown on TV have the same goal, to create an illusion.

This particular ad showed a number of young models wearing tight fitting jeans, slinking their way into view, their backs to the screen. As a slow rhythm was played in the background, the models' well-defined derrieres began to gyrate, thus becoming the sole focus of attention. Not a word was offered about the quality of the jeans, the wearing comfort, or the price, as the gyrating butts faded away in the background.

Well, what's the illusion? The illusion is that if we buy their particular brand of jeans, our buttocks "might" look as well defined as those of the models did. We are fully aware that most members of the human race have been assigned buttocks that are a far cry from a full and pleasant definition. So, the illusion keeps on lingering in the minds of many who hope in the realization of impossible dreams. And if your size of jeans refuses to rise above your knees, take heart, keep pulling and never give up.

During the 1998 Winter Olympics, in Japan, the viewers' attention was continually drawn to a series of vignettes featuring Mercury cars. One of them was particularly baffling to me.

The scene took place in an airport. A man and a woman were talking to one another. A plane was waiting close by. He was staying. She was leaving. It was foggy and both were wearing trench coats. As she was about to board the plane, the man wanted to know if the woman loved him more than she loved her Mercury. As she heard the question, her head went up and she appeared confused. She didn't remember that she owned a Mercury. She was suffering from amnesia. The man appeared perplexed. As she reached the plane's door, she looked at the man, and with a painful look, she asked: "Where am I going?" The man shrugged his shoulders. That was it.

Six years later, I still can't figure out what that ad was about. Could there be a possible link between amnesia and the Mercury cars? What about the fog ? Could it be that the trench coats had something to do with the efficiency of the safety belts? By the way, what ever happened to the Mercury cars? Did the managerial staff come up with a communal attack of amnesia?

Anyway, thank heavens that there are still a few courageous companies left, whose TV ads are fairly easy to grasp. One of those is the Certs Candy, the breath cleaner.

The ad showed a young man who looked dejected. He couldn't get a date because he had bad breath. He decided to try a Certs candy. As soon as he finished it, his problem was over. The following scene showed the young man smiling from ear to ear. He was in the company of several cute girls, who took turns falling all over him.

I felt good for the guy, but I was skeptical about the miraculous power of the candy. So, I decided to investigate the matter personally.

I went to a park and sat on a bench. I had a full roll of Certs with me. I began chewing them up one after the other. I waited for a long time. Not one solitary soul came meandering near the bench I was occupying. Soon enough, I began to experience intestinal spasms, and if that was not enough, a spiteful pigeon decided to relieve himself (herself?) on one of my shoes.

After that unpleasant experience, I stopped buying Certs, and kept my distance from park benches and pigeons too.

THE SPEECH

In the early evening of June 9, 1940, the Italian Radio Network (R.A.I.) interrupted its scheduled program with the following statement:

"Attention! Tomorrow, June 10, at noontime, "Il Duce" will address the nation. All work will stop for the duration of the address. The local authorities will set up loudspeakers in all public squares." The same announcement was repeated every fifteen minutes, until midnight.

The news spread quickly and people began to gather at street corners, bus stops, or wherever they happened to be. They were talking, wondering, speculating as to the reason for the announcement.

Joining the German forces in the war was a primary concern. Such a possibility affected us in different ways. For some, fighting the war under Mussolini's leadership aroused strong passions. For others, the same thought generated feelings of deep concern.

On the morning of the 10th, my mother came knocking at my bedroom door earlier than usual. She wanted to make sure, that I wouldn't be late for school and that I would be properly attired for the event, whatever it was. The day before, the principal of my school, privy to the forthcoming radio announcement, had ordered the staff and the student body to come to school in full uniform.

After the knock at the door, I lingered in bed for a few minutes, wondering about the nature of the announcement. Will it be a declaration of war? Will my two brothers, both in the Navy, be safe? Will we be safe at the home front? Will my mother be able to bear the eventual stress and pain?

A second knock at the door, interrupted my long reverie. Within minutes, I was all dressed up in my "Avanguardista" uniform, consisting of a black shirt, green-gray knee-length shorts, knee-high green-gray socks, black shoes and black cap.

When I swaggered into the kitchen in that black gear, my mother inspected me from head to toe, just to make sure that the uniform was clean. My sister Anna, who didn't seem to be too impressed, looked at me and said: "Are you going to a funeral, little brother?"

After breakfast, I was on my way to school in the company of many of my schoolmates that lived in the neighborhood, all properly attired and emotionally prepared for the unusual occasion. We swaggered down the road chanting party slogans. It felt as though we were going to a sport event or a County Fair, hoping to win a prize.

As we were chanting our way to school, I noticed that the small gatherings of the day before had swelled into small crowds. The disussions had grown louder and more contentious. There were those who, driven by excessive patriotic fervor, felt duty bound to publicly chastise those who dared to voice legitimate feelings of concern. Words such as duty, loyalty, patriotism and even treason were being tossed around, inflaming the passions of many.

As soon as we arrived in the schoolyard, we were directed to join the rest of the student body in the basement of the school, where the gym was located. The place was warm and musty, mercifully alleviated by two rickety ceiling fans.

When the principal walked in, escorted by a uniformed entourage, the noise level quickly subsided. He stood on a wooden platform, immoblile, hands on hips and with a dour expression on his face.

A man in his fifties, he was rather short, pudgy and totally bald. Aware of his physical shortcomings, he tried to compensate with a booming voice and a demeanor that boarded on the theatrical. His name was Filippo Agiglia, a household name in the Fascist circles of Palermo.

He stood in front of us, dressed in his fancy parade uniform of "Comandante Regionale", sporting a headgear adorned with a silky fringe, and a black shirt crowded with several rows of medals and multicolored ribbons. A silky sash over his green-gray riding style pants partially hid his bulging gut. A shiny, knee-high black boots with elevated heels completed his pretentious costume. A leather wand hanging from his side added a measure of bluster to his appearance.

It wasn't easy for a crowd of exuberant teenagers to stay at attention and keep a serious face, while the "Comandante" was staring down on us.

We tried hard to stifle our snickering, but the more we tried the louder it got. Then, the rhythmic screeching of the ceiling fans turned the giggles into peals of laughter. The "Comandante" visibly annoyed, remedied the situation by ordering the entire assembly to stay at attention while reciting the Fascist Credo, a long set of rules governing the proper behavior of the Fascist youth.

It took us twice the normal time to finish the assignment. In the middle of it, someone in the assembly was suddenly afflicted by a coughing fit. It must have been contagious, because within seconds the coughing became an epidemic and the resulting cacophony reached a noisy level unacceptable to the "Comandante."

In fact, when it appeared that he was about ready to pop his cork, he proceeded to retaliate by making us suffer through a lengthy documentary showing the many accomplishments of Fascism, from the 1922 March-on-Rome to the conquest of Ethiopia.

During the presentation, the "Comandante" kept walking up and down the aisles wearing a bristling gaze and trying to elicit our cheers with a wave of his wand.

As noontime approached, we marched off to the soccer field where a large crowd was already seated in the stands. In the middle of it, on a wooden platform, the principal found a stage where he felt free to strut about like a peacock at a Fowl Show.

Exactly at noon, the two loudspeakers mounted at each end of the field came alive. The familiar, shrill voice of Achille Starace, the Party Secretary, came through with his patented introduction: "Comrades, let us salute IL DUCE, the FOUNDER OF THE EMPIRE!" A roar blasted through the loudspeakers, followed by the familiar chant: DU-CE! DU-CE! DU-CE!

When the excitement subsided, there was a pause. Then, filled with emotions, the "Voice" rang out with the dramatic flair most of us had grown accustomed to love:

"Italians, from the Alps to Sicily; Italians, from the Libyan shores to the plains of Ethiopia; Italians who live in foreign lands; sons and daughters of our motherland, listen!

The hour of decision has finally arrived. Today, I have summoned to Palazzo Venezia the ambassadors of Great Britain and France. In their hands, I have placed a declaration of war!"

The crowd burst into a frenzy. The cheering was deafining. The chanting resumed louder than before. At our location, we joined in the general jubilation.

Continuing in his speech, Mussolini reiterated the old theme concerning the right of the Italian nation to secure "a place in the sun" for all its people. He further boasted about the "one million bayonets" that he was ready to contribute to the Axis war effort.

The end of the speech was a stirring call to arms:

"On to victory! On to victory! Over the slavery of oppression and greed. We shall win! We shall win, to give the world a new era of justice and peace."

From the north to the south, from the smallest villages to the largest cities, the cheering continued into the night, reminiscent of an afternoon in the month of July 1982, when the Italian soccer team won the World Cup in Madrid, Spain. Amazing!

After the expected animated discussions, underlined with rosy predictions, wishful speculations and fearful consequences, I finally made it home. My mother and Anna were teary-eyed and in a somber mood. A photo of my two brothers, together, and in Navy uniforms, was prominently displayed on the kitchen table.

The feeling of extravagant euphoria that I had shared with my schoolmates a short time before, was completely gone and so was the echo of the wild cheering. Suddenly, my mind felt numb and somber thoughts began to crowd it.

It was the afternoon of June 10, 1940. World War II had just begun.

THE ABUSE OF FREEDOM

Often times, we, Americans, are reminded here at home, more out of a spirit of controversy than a sense of national pride, that we live in the Land of the Free.

We have come to believe that freedom is the birthright of all Americans, an indelible mark of our identity, the defining attribute of who we are.

Sometimes, in the course of our daily life, we casually bandy the word freedom around, more to assert our rights than to remind ourselves of the serious responsibilities that the word entails. In so doing, the noble concept of freedom loses some of its luster, and its meaning becomes garbled as we rush to use it as a convenient means to achieve our selfish ends.

If we were to read the historic accounts of all nations, we would probably find that freedom was the battle cry that rallied oppressed people into a battlefield, it was the banner to fight under, the noblest idea to die for. After centuries of oppression and want, for many around the world, still today, freedom remains an improbable dream.

On July 4, 1776, some wise men, with noble minds and righteous spirits, America's Founding Fathers, blessed by the Almighty God, appeared on the American Horizon, and together created the premise for the realization of the improbable dream. They spoke loudly and clearly the words the people everywhere dreamt to hear:

"WE HOLD THESE TRUTHS TO BE SELF-EVIDENT, THAT ALL MEN ARE CREATED EQUAL, THAT THEY ARE ENDOWED BY THEIR CREATOR WITH CERTAIN UNALIENABLE RIGHTS, THAT AMONG THESE ARE LIFE, LIBERTY AND THE PURSUIT OF HAPPINESS."

Those men of faith believed in a loving and generous God, who endowed His creatures with fundamental rights, without which life cannot prosper.

Those among us who seek to honor and preserve our unalienable rights must honor truth above all. That is to say that in order for us to enjoy the fruits of our freedom, we must conclude that the rights we have been endowed with must be exerted within the limits set forth by Almighty God, the originator of the endowment. Such limits must include a compelling duty on our part to exercise a keen sense of personal responsibility that allows us to pursue truth and justice in everything we say and do. Freedom exercised in a climate of wanton irresponsibility becomes licentiousness. Anyone who dares to invoke his/her rights without regard to truth and justice negates the very essence of freedom and puts in jeopardy its very existence.

In recent years, particularly the last decade, we have witnessed within our country a seemingly organized assault against the moral and spiritual values upon which the strength of our nation rests. Basic virtues, such as honor, fairness, justice, compassion, truthfulness, to mention a few, once recognized as indispensable characteristics of one's human worth, seem to have lost much of their luster, if not their meaning.

Let us consider the mass media of today and the kind of freedom they believe in. They are in charge of newspapers, magazines, radio stations, film studios, TV stations and Internet websites.

They are all business people, and as we all know business people stay in business for one reason alone: To make money, lots of it. Therefore, all they write, say or show is meticulously designed to please their specific audiences. The content of what they offer is largely protected by the First Amendment of our Constitution under the guise of freedom of speech.

Even though today's mass media refuse to acknowledge even a minimal share of responsibility in the fact that they, in all they write, in all they say and in all they show and do, contribute in a considerable way to the shaping of beliefs, the setting of attitudes and the influencing of behavioral standards of society at large.

It is, however, an accepted conclusion shared by many respected psychologists that the mass media did play, and still do play, a large part in affecting our young people in particular, in the ways they should think and act.

Fair people who seek the truth do not need to listen to professional points of view or see the results of polls to arrive at the disturbing truth. They only need to look at the questionable contents of most of the films coming out of Hollywood, whose scripts are steeped in senseless violence, scurrilous language and a brazen display of unrestrained lust.

No, this is not the way to assure the proper moral growth of our children. The shows that our young people need to watch are those that are geared to teach compassion, generosity, moral integrity and individual responsibility, virtues these that please God and honor family and country. Our youth needs to be shown how to choose between what is good and what feels good, between what's important and what's frivolous. They need to know that wealth, power, fame, physical beauty are not the standards that define a successful life.

Pope John Paul II. one of the wisest and holiest men of the present era, during his speech delivered at the United Nation General Assembly in New York, defined freedom as follows:

"True freedom does not give people the right to do what they want. It only gives them the right to do what they "ought." The want is usually governed by irresponsibility and greed, while the "ought" is always understood and nurtured within the realm of God's laws.

It is clear, that those who are responsible for the programs shown on the television networks fail to see the obvious difference, therefore they keep cranking up, on a daily basis, talk-shows and sit-coms whose contents are purposely designed to offend the basic tenets of human decency.

Watching the quality of the shows they offer, one must conclude that profits are the only reason for doing what they do; the profits, by the way, are directly proportional to the amount of violence and sexually arousing situations that they bring to the screen. G-movies don't create profits, R-movies do. Therefore, the greater the violence and the more titillating the sexual scenes, the more attention are able to arouse and, consequently more profits they will be able to reap.

The Internet is the latest arrival in the race for easy bucks. Those responsible are in the pursuit of easy profit by exploiting a grubby human weakness: pornography. Teenagers are not free from it. They only need a valid charge card to be infected for life.

Recently, the U.S. Supreme Court in a 5-4 decision, allowed the pornographers to continue their business undisturbed. They cannot be denied their right to free speech. Amazing! Nowadays, selling porn on the Internet is defined by five of our Supremes as a "right to free speech." Incredible, but true!

To all the people of America, who have the courage to stand up and raise their voices in defense of our moral values, those entrepreneurs who make their millions by selling moral poison and social garbage keep echoing the same tune:

"We make what sells! We give the public what they want! The parents are the guardians of their children! We don't moralize! We have the right to free speech! Indeed!

What ever happened to the old saying: God, country and family?

This country was founded by men who believed in God, honored Him and obeyed His laws.

"In God We Trust," "One nation Under God," "America! America! God shed His graces on thee!" These words are not a figment of someone's imagination. No, these are expressions, true and real, intimately connected with the soul of America.

I clearly remember that on March 31, 1953, when I became an American Citizen, and for the first time I recited the Pledge of Allegiance, tears started to flow down my cheeks, tears of pride, tears of gratitude, and tears of praise to Almighty God, who allowed my dream to become a reality.

Many times, I have asked myself these simple questions: " Why is it that now our God, the God of our Fathers, is being pushed out of our existence? Why is it that The Ten Commandments, the precepts of our faith, the faith of our Fathers, are now considered an embarrassment to some? If they are considered to be so much of an embarrassment, why are they so prominently displayed in the Supreme Court Building? In fact, inside the courtroom, right above where the Justices sit, the Ten Commandments are gloriously displayed, for all to see.

Evidently, among many others, even the Supreme Court Justices fail to pay attention to the Divine Guidance that's so visible anywhere they look. In fact, in 1973, five Justices out of nine, in the infamous Roe vs. Wade controversial case granted to all the American women the "right to privacy" and as result of that decision, also the right to abort pregnancies within the first trimester of gestation. Evidently, the five Justices responsible for that incredible moral blunder never had the time or the willingness to read aloud to themselves the fifth of the Ten Commandments, which clearly warns: **YOU SHALL NOT KILL!**

Other reasonable questions come to mind. "Are moral principles no longer viable in our modern society? And if they are, why is it that those in position of power don't seem to care? Shouldn't the First Amendment protect all citizens? Or just those who intend to abuse it.

Shouldn't our elected officials pay more attention to the needs of their constituencies? Or should they spend most of their time discussing important issues with the lobbyists.

The Bill of Rights was not conceived to become a convenient tool to be used to assert or defend personal agendas, nor was it intended to facilitate the safe pursuit of immoral aims. The Bill of Rights was conceived, voted and passed to be just that, a bill to defend the rights of all citizens, rights based on fairness and justice. Freedom thrives on fairness and justice. It withers, when it's abused or exploited.

When freedom becomes merely a convenient tool and a rallying cry in the pursuit of questionable causes; when freedom is used as an instrument that preys on the mind of the adolescent, or as a means to titillate the prurient penchant of the weak-willed; when freedom is abused to justify irresponsible behavior, and becomes a lance for the foolhardy or a shield for the coward, then freedom is reduced to a meaningless expression, just a word without power and appeal.

No, this is not the kind of freedom our ancestors envisioned. The freedom worth cherishing is the same one they cherished, the kind that allows us to walk unafraid in the light of God's truth, and let's us bask in the fairness of His justice.

ABOUT THE AUTHOR

Joseph Cione is a retired foreign languages teacher, who taught French, Spanish and Italian in the New York City public school system. His career spanned almost a quarter of a century.

The author enjoyed writing poems since his school years in Sicily. A dozen of his poems written in Italian were published during the 1991-92 period in "AMERICA OGGI," a daily, popular publication in Italian, sold in the greater New Work area.

Two of his poems, in English, were published in 1999, in the monthly magazine "Queen of Hearts" that has a wide circulation in Long Island, N.Y.

This is the first book of poems published by the author, following two books of memoirs, recently published by Author House: "Sicily On My Mind" and "Yearning to Breathe Free"

Printed in the United States
23953LVS00005BA/235-243